B O O K   R E V I E W S

Here's what people are saying:

The images and rhythms are energetic and unusual, and the sheer nonsensical and offbeat aspects will delight some readers.
from KIRKUS REVIEWS

The illustrations add fun and pleasure to the poems.
from THE GEORGE C. STONE CENTER FOR CHILDREN'S BOOKS

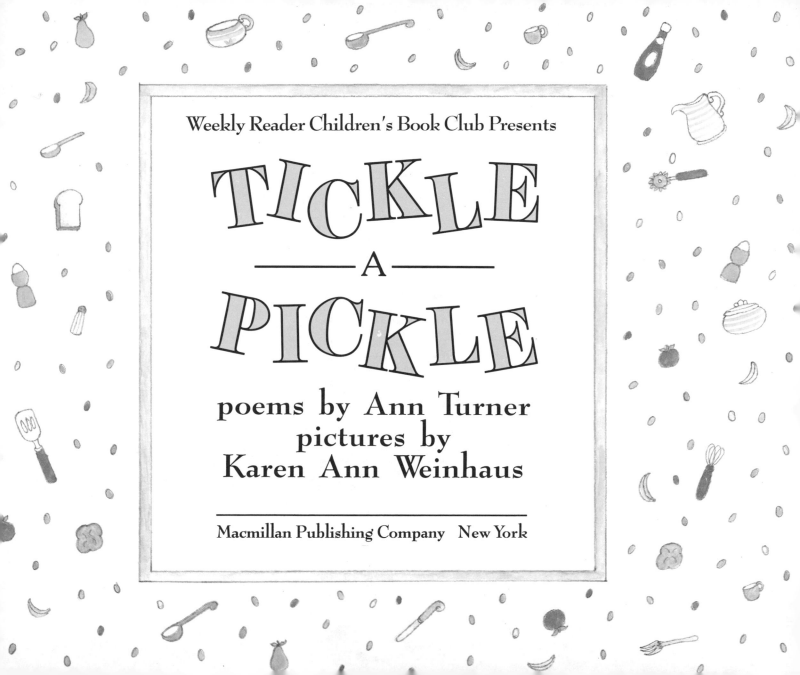

Weekly Reader Children's Book Club Presents

TICKLE
— A —
PICKLE

poems by Ann Turner
pictures by
Karen Ann Weinhaus

Macmillan Publishing Company New York

This book is a presentation of Weekly Reader Books.
Weekly Reader Books offers book clubs for children
from preschool through high school. For further
information write to: **Weekly Reader Books,**
4343 Equity Drive, Columbus, Ohio 43228.

This edition is published by arrangement with
Four Winds Press, an imprint of
The Macmillan Publishing Company,
a Division of Macmillan, Inc.
Weekly Reader is a federally registered
trademark of Field Publications.
Weekly Reader Books edition printed in the
United States of America.

Macmillan Publishing Company
866 Third Avenue, New York, N.Y. 10022
Collier Macmillan Canada, Inc.
Printed and bound by South China Printing Company, Hong Kong
First American Edition
10   9   8   7   6   5   4   3   2   1
The text of this book is set in 18 pt. Cloister.
The illustrations are rendered in pencil and watercolor and
reproduced in full color.
Library of Congress Cataloging-in-Publication Data
Turner, Ann Warren.
Tickle a pickle.
Summary: Nineteen poems including such titles as
"Spaghetti for One Thousand," "Horrendous, Gorrendous,"
and "Lucky You."
1. Children's poetry, American. [1. American
poetry]. I. Weinhaus, Karen Ann, ill. II. Title.
PS3570.U665T5   1986   811'.54   85-18847
ISBN 0-02-789280-8

For Josh and Sarah
with love
—A.T.

To my cousins Babs and Larry Armour
and Gerry and Sharon Keller
—K.A.W.

TICKLE A PICKLE

Tickle a pickle,   greet a beet,   say "eek!" to a leek,

put a slipper on the pepper,   invite a pea to tea,

marry the potatoes and tomatoes,

take a melon to a felon,

watch a corn born,

cut the bunions from an onion,

burp a turnip,

pardon the garden.

SPAGHETTI FOR ONE THOUSAND

Make a bonfire from tires,
use an empty truck for a pot,
pour in half a lake,
and wait for it to bubble.

Throw in ten cases of pasta,
stir it with a crane,
don't take it out
till it's done al dente.

Only problem is,
you forgot the sauce!

CLONE

I dreamed I had a clone,
    Richard E. Powers Turner,
who went to school, did all my work,
    and listened to that boring drone.

I dreamed I had a clone,
    (I kept him in my closet)
for rainy days or dentist days,
    and having to visit Aunt Moan.

I dreamed I had a clone,
but I'd never let him out—

for hot jam sandwiches, space war movies,
or the dark end of day coming home.

HORRENDOUS, GORRENDOUS

Horrendous, gorrendous Mary Jane Kline
ate all the pickles and drank all the wine.
First she turned green, then she turned red.
They hosed her down and sent her to bed.

Horrendous, gorrendous Mary Jane Kline
stole everyone's bike in split-second time.
They found them piled inside her house,
the one stuffed with garbage and half a dead mouse.

Horrendous, gorrendous Mary Jane Kline
climbed up houses on long trailing vines.

She hid powdered soap under the beds,
and once when it rained, the suds choked a man dead.

Horrendous, gorrendous Mary Jane Kline
who cares what she does or whether it rhymes.
Take her away, put her in jail,
make her eat rutabagas raw from a pail.

VISITING

They all sit in a row
   and talk and talk and talk,
no one plays ball, no one jumps rope,
   they're tired as tired old toes.

They complain of green mold
   on the new bathroom walls,
all the things I do wrong,
   and the chill winter cold.

Why not hide in the barn
   and tell bad terrible jokes,
climb a tall tree, bury a doll
   and practice fire alarms.

They still sit in a row,
   and open and shut their mouths,
someone's snoring long and loud,
   they're tired as tired old toes!

QUEEN OF THE NIGHT

I never suck my thumb
　　at night
or jump into bed when you turn out the light.

I never look in the closet
　　for witches
or shiver and shake at the thought of glitches.

I never carry a flashlight
   down the hall
or sing out loud like a woman at a ball.

   I never suck my thumb,

I'm queen of
   the night

and I make my own light.

MAGIC

A sorcerer has scarves up his sleeves,
a mouse in his ear,
a hundred violins in his hand.

He can dance with the moon,

skip stones over stars,

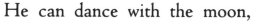

and roll night up in a bag.

But most of the time he sits at home,
sitting and growing his nose.

JOSHUA'S HAT

Joshua's hat has silver wings;
  he flies upside down,
does loop-de-loops,
  goes round the room
and up to town.

When he takes
   it off at night,
it glides up walls
   and bumps the window
like a bird trying to get out.

Joshua's hat
   is something special
and it only works for him.

JUMPING ROPE RHYME

Marmalade pajamas,
  peanut butter hats,
eat our clothes, munch our clothes
  washing's just for cats.

Onion pizza parkas,
  sweet potato jeans,
mash our clothes, crunch our clothes
  make them jelly beans.

Melted butter sweaters,
  drippy ice cream shoes,
sip our clothes, slurp our clothes
  that's what we should do.

BIRDBATH

Put a tiny bar of soap
and the slightest slip of cloth
by the bubble bath for birds.
Set a thimble of champagne
by the smallest record ever.
Splash in time to the tunes.

LUCKY YOU

I'm Batman with a flying cape

and he's Robin
of five hundred
magical escapes

and you can be my dog.

MAKING SOUP

We are making toilet soup,

putting in my father's shoes!

First a dash of talcum powder,
then a shake of oil,

stir with the johnny mop,

stir,   stir,   stir!

Then we hear quick footsteps
coming down the hall,
put away the cooking tools,
   put away the spice,
cook's gone home—
   soup's done just right!

PETER MESS

Peter's in the bathroom
fixing up a mess,
I can hear the paper roll
rattling on the wall.

Peter's busy making
a spider web inside,
toilet paper spinning out
from hooks and walls and doors.

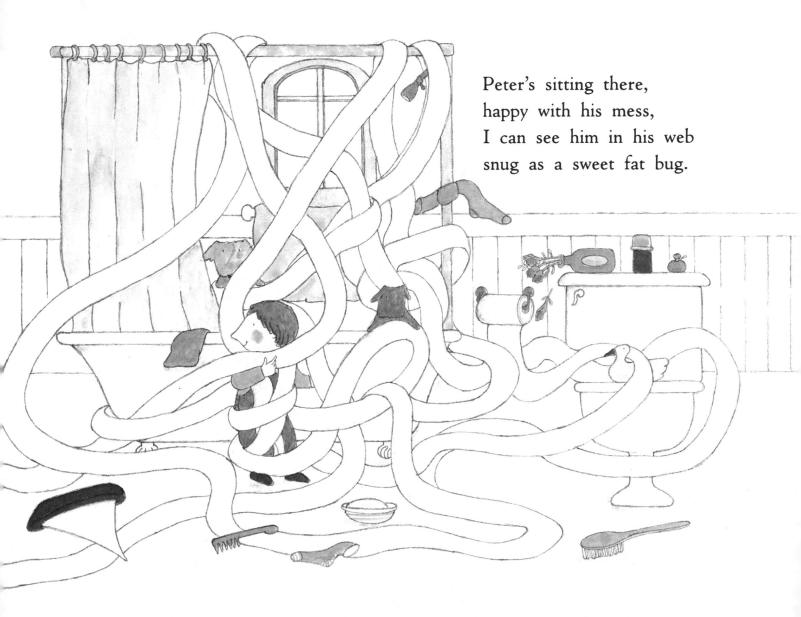

Peter's sitting there,
happy with his mess,
I can see him in his web
snug as a sweet fat bug.

SPRING BATH

Chocolate ice cream on my cheeks
ice cream on my neck,
dribble it dribble it down to the belt,
watch it go all over my toes.

Chocolate ice cream gums my nose
now it's in my hair,
it's a bath I take each spring
the very best all year.

Taste it outside with your tongue

taste it inside upside down

chocolate ice cream, it's a bath,

the very best all year.

ELSIE PERRELLI

Elsie Perrelli went to the beach
with a pail and a digging stick.
Her brother brought a peach.

Elsie Perrelli went to the beach
with a pail and a digging stick,
a spade and two hefty picks.
Her brother brought a peach and a leash.

Elsie Perrelli went to the beach
with a pail and a digging stick,
a spade and two hefty picks,
one wheelbarrow and a bulldozer.
Her brother brought a peach,
a leash and some ceviche.

Elsie Perrelli went to the beach
with a pail and a digging stick,
a spade and two hefty picks,
one wheelbarrow and a bulldozer,
and a truck and a front loader.
Her brother brought a peach, a leash,
some ceviche, and an onion quiche.

Elsie Perrelli went to the beach
with a pail and a digging stick,
a spade and two hefty picks,
one wheelbarrow and a bulldozer,
a truck and a front loader,
and a burly crew of eighty-six.
Her brother stayed at home,
peeled the peach,
put down the leash,
ate the ceviche
and the onion quiche.

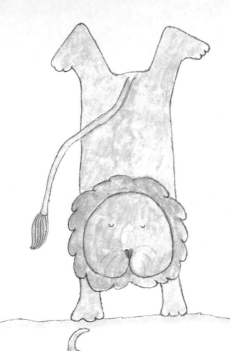

WHAT THE ANIMALS DO

The lion frequently stands on his head,
"To balance my mane, don't you see."

The hippo does cartwheels, ten in a row,
"To settle my stomach," says she.

Giraffes always jump on tall pogo sticks,
"It shortens my neck to a T."

But alligators climb up high in the trees,
and cheerily say, "Come see me."

GARDEN DELIVERY

Mail a snail
in a soft, green leaf,

stamp it
with pollen from a bee,

tuck it
deep inside the peony

the cricket
snugs it under his arm,

carries it
under the foxglove bells

delivers it
to the door of the mole

who unwraps it
and dines on snail with garlic.

RELATIVES

He's got his uncle's eyes,
his aunty's nose,
grandma's ears
and grandpa's mouth.

If that is so,
how does uncle see
or aunty smell?
How does grandma hear
or grandpa speak?

Relatives must be
some kind of cannibals.

PAPERWEIGHT

There's an ant-sized farm with pin-sized windows
and a path like thread where green trees grow.
When the sun goes out and the snow comes down,
a tiny man runs out and shovels with a frown.